P9-CAA-094

Weird and Wonderful
Attack and Defense

KINGFISHER
LONDON & NEW YORK

Published in the United States by Kingfisher,
175 Fifth Ave., New York, NY 10010

Kingfisher is an imprint of Macmillan
Children's Books, London.
All rights reserved.

Distributed in the U.S. by Macmillan,
175 Fifth Ave., New York, NY 10010

Library of Congress Cataloging-in-Publication
data has been applied for.

Kingfisher books are available for special
promotions and premiums. For details contact:
Special Markets Department, Macmillan,
175 Fifth Ave., New York, NY 10010.

For more information, please visit
www.kingfisherbooks.com

Conceived and produced by
Weldon Owen Pty Ltd
59–61 Victoria Street, McMahons Point
Sydney NSW 2060, Australia
weldonowenpublishing.com

Copyright © 2011 Weldon Owen Pty Ltd

WELDON OWEN PTY LTD
Managing Director Kay Scarlett
Publisher Corinne Roberts
Creative Director Sue Burk
**Senior Vice President,
International Sales** Stuart Laurence
Sales Manager, North America Ellen Towell
**Administration Manager,
International Sales** Kristine Ravn

Managing Editor Helen Bateman
Consultant Professor Phil Whitfield
Design Concept Cooling Brown Ltd
Designer Michelle Cutler
Images Manager Trucie Henderson
Production Director Todd Rechner
Production and Prepress Controller Mike Crowton

All rights reserved. No part of this publication may be
reproduced, stored in a retrieval system, or transmitted
in any form or by any means, electronic, mechanical,
photocopying, recording, or otherwise, without the
permission of the copyright holder and publisher.

ISBN: 978-0-7534-6723-7

Printed and bound in China by 1010 Printing Int Ltd.

The paper used in the manufacture of this book is
sourced from wood grown in sustainable forests.
It complies with the Environmental Management
System Standard ISO 14001:2004

A WELDON OWEN PRODUCTION

© 2011 Discovery Communications, LLC.
Animal Planet and the Animal Planet logo
are trademarks of Discovery Communications,
LLC, used under license. All rights reserved.

animalplanet.com
animalplanetbooks.com

Weird and Wonderful

Attack and Defense

Kathy Riley

Astonishing Animals

Bizarre Behavior

KINGFISHER

NEW YORK

Contents

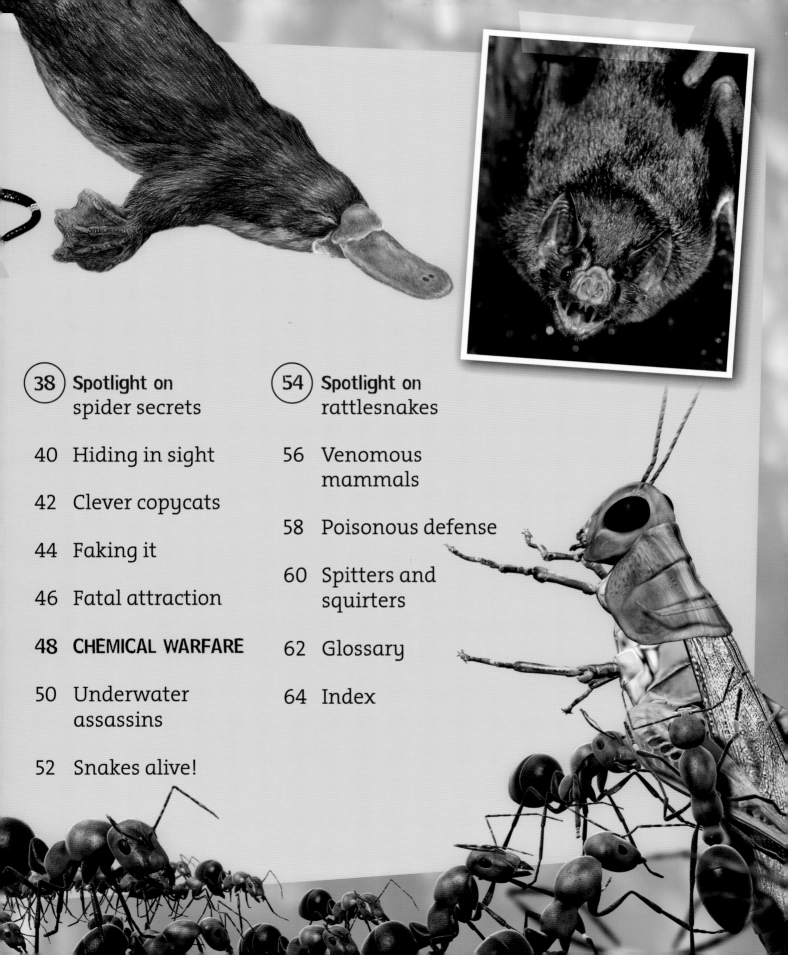

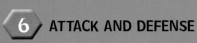

WEAPONS AND TOOLS

Animals are equipped with a variety of built-in weapons and tools to help them survive: from razor-sharp teeth and claws, impenetrable body armor, and powerful muscles to toxic saliva, electricity, and poisonous body parts. These weapons and tools can make even the smallest creature a formidable and deadly opponent.

A long-tailed pangolin shows off its body armor.

Jaws of death

Chomping, chewing, puncturing, tearing, grinding, and cutting—these are just a few of the tasks that predatory animals need their teeth and jaws to perform. Their teeth come in all shapes and sizes, each specially designed for its job. Some animals' mouths have extra hidden weapons, such as deadly saliva.

Shark attack

The great white shark has the largest and most fearsome teeth of all the world's sharks. Each tooth is serrated and as sharp as a saw blade.

A great white shark lunges up from below, its massive teeth bared and ready to bite down on its prey.

Dirty tricks The Komodo dragon is the world's largest lizard. Its deadliest weapon is the bacteria in its saliva. Once bitten, the dragon's prey slowly dies of blood poisoning.

Specialized teeth A tiger has big canine teeth for killing, small front incisors for plucking feathers or fur, and cheek teeth for ripping meat off bones and chomping it into chunks.

Animal facts

1 Dolphins keep the same set of teeth for their whole lives.

2 Tusks are very long teeth. About one third of an elephant's tusk is hidden inside its head.

3 A shark is continually growing new sets of teeth. Every time the shark loses a tooth, a new one moves forward to take its place.

Nifty fingers

We would be lost without the use of our fingers and hands, and so would many other creatures in the animal kingdom. Whether they are needed for slashing, grasping, climbing, digging, cutting, plucking, or piercing, animals' claws and talons are vitally important for their survival.

Powerful grasp An owl swoops down with toes and sharp talons ready to close around its victim. Its feet can lock in and hold prey for hours without tiring.

Hungry bear Grizzly bears use their strong claws to dig into burrows; strike down large animals such as moose; pluck fish from rivers; and forage for insects, fruits, and plants.

Nail it Shown here in real size, a bear's claw is powerful and versatile. It can perform many different jobs—from holding and digging to cutting, ripping, and slashing.

← 4 inches (10 cm) →

Big, powerful, crushing claws

Slender fingers and sharp nails

Designer digits

Whether performing delicate tasks such as picking berries and extracting insects, or destructive jobs such as crushing prey, animals' claws are cleverly designed to meet their needs.

Pincer attack Lobsters have oversized crusher claws and smaller pincer claws for attacking and tearing apart their prey.

Insect excavator The aye-aye from Madagascar has a long, spindly middle finger for extracting grubs from tree holes.

Rock star The marine iguana, which is found along the coast of the Galápagos Islands, has long, curved claws, which help it grip on to rocks in heavy seas.

 ## Animal facts

1 The osprey, a type of raptor, can reverse its outer toe to allow it to grab and carry a fish using two claws in front and two behind.

2 A lobster can drop a claw and grow back another one.

3 Koalas and some primates, including humans and gorillas, are the only animals with fingerprints.

Creepy-crawly A centipede is small, but ferocious. It is carnivorous and has poisonous claws behind its mouth that can trap and paralyze prey.

little monsters

In the animal kingdom, small does not necessarily mean weak. Poison, camouflage, well-developed senses, and finely tuned physical characteristics are just some of the weapons these miniature hunters use to rule their domain. Sometimes being small is a great advantage in itself, as it means escaping detection until the last possible moment.

Sting operation Scorpions are menacing creatures with large, snapping pincers and a stinging tail that whips around to deliver a fatal dose of poison to small animals.

Mighty pincers trap or crush prey in their grasp.

Ambush artist Folding its spiny forelegs as if in prayer, the praying mantis sits camouflaged on a branch until an unsuspecting victim approaches. Then it pounces with fierce precision.

Funnel-web spider

With solid, black, hairy bodies, aggressive natures, and fangs as sharp and deadly as pickaxes, Australia's funnel-web spiders are among the most dangerous and venomous spiders in the world.

Attack mode This funnel-web spider is ready to strike. It cannot see with its head back; instead, it responds to vibrations. Its venom contains a chemical called atracotoxin, which can kill humans.

The pedipalps, next to the mouth, aid in eating food.

Deadly venom travels through ducts in the fangs.

Tiny hairs on the spider's body pick up smells, sounds, and vibrations.

The **big** squeeze

Pythons and boas are the largest living snakes in the world, and they have a unique method of attack: they wrap their long body around prey and use their powerful muscles to squeeze it to death. Then they eat their victim whole. Digesting a large animal can take weeks or even months.

Quick lunge The emerald tree boa from South America catches prey with its long teeth, pulls it in, and then asphyxiates it.

Last gasp

Contrary to what many people think, constrictors do not kill their prey by crushing it. Rather, they tighten their grip every time the victim breathes out. Gradually, the victim suffocates.

The Amazon tree boa anchors itself around a tree branch, leaving its front end free to strike out at prey.

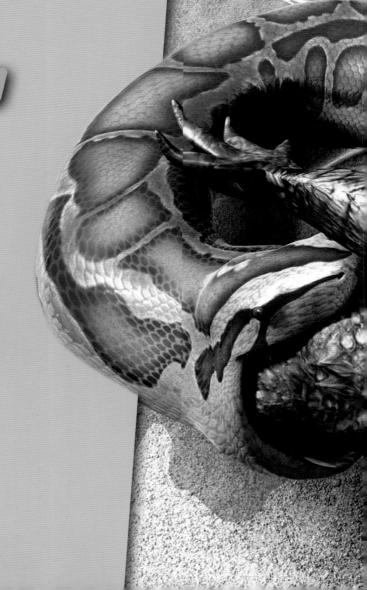

Death hug A young Siamese crocodile is no match for a hungry Burmese python. These pythons can grow to 20 feet (6 m) and weigh 100 pounds (45 kg).

What is the main difference between a python and a boa?

Animal facts

1 Pythons and boas are the only snakes with remnant hind limbs. These limbs are known as anal spurs.

2 The longest snake in the world is the reticulated python, which regularly reaches lengths of more than 20½ feet (6.25 m).

3 Pythons and boas move the bones in their jaws apart to eat their prey whole.

A: A boa gives birth to live young, whereas a python lays eggs.

Suits of armor

Sometimes the best defense is an impenetrable outer layer—one that is so tough an attacker soon gives up and moves on to an easier target. Spikes, shells, scales, and thick hides are a few examples of the body armor worn by animals to protect them from predators.

Spines move to help urchins change direction.

Prickly customer
Sea urchins belong to a group called echinoderms, from the Greek word for "spiny-skinned." Many sea urchin species have venom in their spines for extra protection.

Body armor The armadillo's head and back are covered with a flexible carapace of bony plates covered with horny skin. Its belly, however, is soft and vulnerable.

Pangolin protection

A pangolin, also known as a scaly anteater, has very sharp scales. When attacked, it will roll into a tight ball that is almost impossible to unroll.

Although it looks like a reptile, a pangolin is actually a mammal.

Overlapping scales

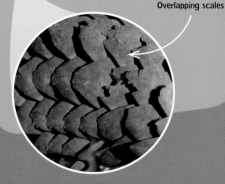

Little bug The wood louse is sometimes called the armadillo bug because of its resemblance to a tiny armadillo. It is a land-dwelling crustacean.

ZOOM IN

Watch out, these spines can hurt!

All puffed up Puffer fish defend themselves by inflating with water or air to try to appear larger. Their spines are stiff, pointed, and very sharp.

Each spine is sharp and hollow.

Spiky hairdo An echidna's spines are actually modified hairs. When threatened, it will curl into a ball or burrow into the ground.

Horned and dangerous A rhinoceros's horn is made up of fibrous keratin. This, together with its incredibly tough skin, makes it very well protected.

Blood thirsty

These creatures might be small, but they are perfectly designed for finding and feasting on their favorite food: blood! Many carry anesthetic in their saliva, so the host animal does not feel them until they have had their fill. Some are harmless, but some carry diseases that can be dangerous to humans.

Bleeding machine Leeches are mighty clever at getting their meals—chemicals in their saliva stop their host's blood from clotting. This helps increase blood flow and anesthetize the bite site, so they can feast in peace.

One tick can lay up to 3,000 eggs!

An adult bedbug is about the size of an apple seed.

Animal facts

1 A tick can ingest up to 100 times its own body weight in blood.

2 Leeches are sometimes used on human patients, to help reduce swelling and restore blood flow after microsurgery.

3 Only adult female mosquitoes bite humans and other animals. Male mosquitoes feed on nectar and other sources of sugar.

Human hitchhikers Bedbugs and ticks love human blood. Bedbugs can cause rashes and itchy bites, whereas ticks are more dangerous, sometimes carrying diseases or causing paralysis in animals.

A bedbug's skin-piercing mouthparts

Fish parasite

The candiru is a tiny catfish from the Amazon. It swims in through the gills of other fish and feeds on their blood. It can also swim up the urethra of a bathing human!

Little Dracula Vampire bats are found in the Americas, where they hunt at night for warm-blooded animals. Rather than sucking blood, they bite prey then lick blood from the wound.

Vampire bats sometimes feed on human blood!

Shocking hunters

Electricity is used by many animals for a number of different purposes. Some fish use echolocation—they emit pulses that set up an electric field in the water. They use these pulses to work out where their prey is. Others use electric signals to communicate with each other. Many will use electricity to deliver a nasty shock that can stun or kill.

Stargazer fish If you spot this strange face in the sandy seabed, do not touch it. Poisonous spines behind the stargazer's pectoral fins can deliver electric shocks.

 Animal facts

1 Electroreception works better for aquatic animals because water conducts electricity more effectively than air.

2 Sharks detect the electrical fields of potential prey using pores beneath their snout, called the ampullae of Lorenzini.

3 The biggest recorded shock produced by an electric eel is 650 volts, enough to stun a horse.

What is the most electric animal in the world?

A marbled torpedo ray arches its back, ready to deliver a shock.

Electric navigation

All animals produce electrical impulses, but not all animals can sense them. Electroreception is the word used to describe the ability to detect electrical fields, which animals do using special nerves called electroreceptors.

Stun gun This bulls-eye electric ray is one of 40 species of electric rays that stun prey by delivering electric shocks from organs behind their eyes.

The platypus and echidna are the only mammals that can detect electric signals. The platypus has thousands of electroreceptors in its bill.

Powerful shock Electric eels have electricity-generating organs running along the sides of their body. They can produce about 400 volts—enough to knock over a human.

Electroreceptors in the echidna's little snout can pick up minute electric pulses produced by moving prey.

TEAM SPIRIT

Survival is a game of numbers for many animals. When they join forces, they increase their chance of finding food and mates and avoiding attack. Whether it is a graceful pod of dolphins or a seething horde of army ants, a coordinated team of animals is a force to be reckoned with.

Common dolphins live in large groups as a defense against predators.

Pack attack

One wolf is no match for a massive moose, but eight wolves make a truly fearsome team. Many animals—in particular canids, or doglike carnivores—often work together to mount effective and lethal attacks against prey. Sometimes two different species will team up, each bringing their own unique talents to the group.

Strategic hunt Wolves are far more effective at hunting large prey if they work together. A mother caribou cannot defend herself and her calf against a coordinated attack.

Tag teams A pride of lions brings down the prey. Once the lions have finished eating, a pack of hyenas arrives to finish the job.

The wolves stealthily sneak up on the caribou without being seen.

After giving chase, the wolves pinpoint the caribou calf as their chosen target.

Panicked and confused, the caribou calf tries to run and is caught by the wolves.

Animal facts

1 Wolves can run as fast as 40 miles (64 km) per hour over short distances.

2 African hunting dogs roam in packs of up to 40 members.

3 Dog packs have a strict social hierarchy, with an alpha, or top, male and female. The alpha dogs are the only ones allowed to breed.

Team effort Gray wolves will tirelessly chase a moose until it falters. Then they attack swiftly, each wolf biting a different part of the doomed animal.

Water warfare

Whales, dolphins, and porpoises, which belong to the order Cetacea, are highly sociable animals. They have a wide variety of intelligent methods for hunting in groups, which are mesmerizing to watch. From a slippery school of fish to a formidable great white shark, no challenge is too great for these determined teams!

Synchronized swimmers

Dolphins work together to catch a school of fish. One dolphin swims in circles around the school, herding it toward the other dolphins, who are waiting for their fishy feast.

A pod of hungry dolphins works together to make an easy meal out of this large school of fish.

Animal facts

1 A pod of humpback whales can perform bubblenet feeding, where they create a tightening "net" of bubbles around a school of fish, before devouring them.

2 Grouper fish and moray eels hunt cooperatively for prey. Groupers chase prey in the open ocean; when the prey hides in a crevice, the eels flush them out.

3 Common dolphins can form very large groups of sometimes thousands at a time.

A lone great white is no match for a pod of orcas.

Killer move Intelligent and deadly, a pod of orcas, or killer whales, can overcome a great white shark by driving it to the surface and immobilizing it by flipping it upside down.

The 5½-foot (1.7-m) Humboldt squid hunts in groups of up to 1,200 for small fish and krill.

Mob mentality

An immense group of animals is a dramatic and spectacular sight. A swarm of krill can cover 3 miles (5 km) of ocean, flocks of tropical birds make noisy and colorful clouds, and insects often congregate in mind-boggling numbers. Animals swarm to increase their chance of surviving, mating, or feeding.

ZOOM IN

Piranha frenzy Churning water and the flash of scales is all you will see when piranhas attack in a large group, all biting their prey at the same time.

Brutal bite Powerful jaws and razor-sharp teeth can shred the flesh of large prey in minutes. Native South American people use piranha teeth to make weapons and tools.

Midges on the move

If you see a thick cloud of midges hovering midair, it is mating season. Male midges congregate to attract females, who mate with them and then leave to lay their eggs.

Midges usually swarm at dusk during warmer months.

Why do bees swarm?

Locust army A swarm of locusts can travel up to 310 miles (500 km) in one night, descending in their millions and stripping foliage from vast areas.

A: To protect the queen bee when moving to a new nest.

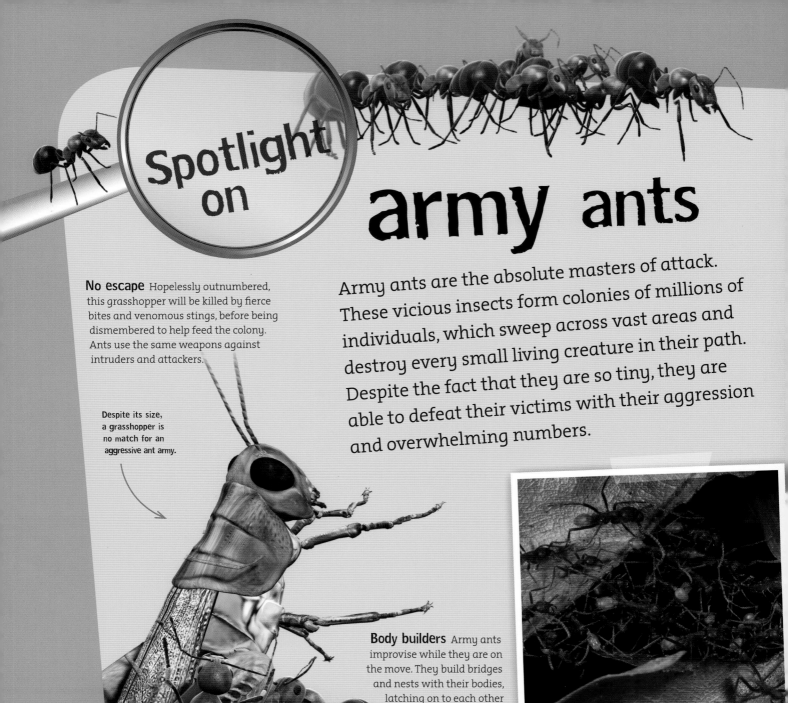

Spotlight on

army ants

Army ants are the absolute masters of attack. These vicious insects form colonies of millions of individuals, which sweep across vast areas and destroy every small living creature in their path. Despite the fact that they are so tiny, they are able to defeat their victims with their aggression and overwhelming numbers.

No escape Hopelessly outnumbered, this grasshopper will be killed by fierce bites and venomous stings, before being dismembered to help feed the colony. Ants use the same weapons against intruders and attackers.

Despite its size, a grasshopper is no match for an aggressive ant army.

Body builders Army ants improvise while they are on the move. They build bridges and nests with their bodies, latching on to each other with their mandibles, or mouthparts, and claws.

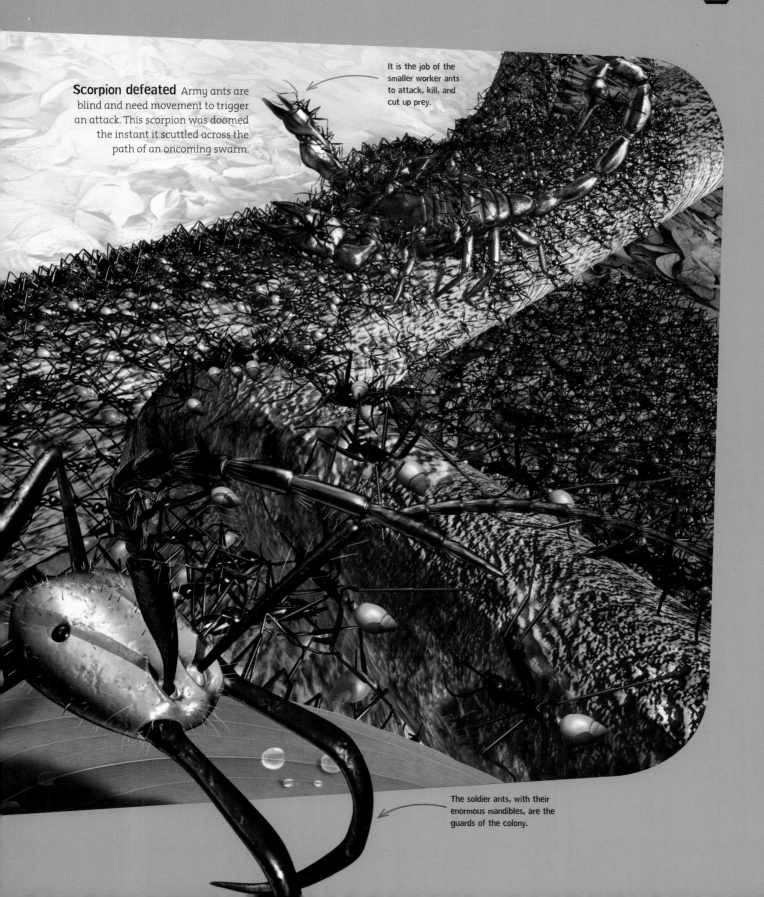

Scorpion defeated Army ants are blind and need movement to trigger an attack. This scorpion was doomed the instant it scuttled across the path of an oncoming swarm.

It is the job of the smaller worker ants to attack, kill, and cut up prey.

The soldier ants, with their enormous mandibles, are the guards of the colony.

Safety in numbers

Animals are usually safer when they stick together. A zebra has less chance of becoming dinner for a hungry lion if it travels in a group. More pairs of eyes mean more chance of spotting trouble, which is important for fish swimming in murky water or animals made vulnerable by feeding or breeding.

All ashore Sea lions hunt individually but form huge colonies when breeding. A group of seals, sea lions, or walrus is called a herd, and a breeding colony is called a rookery.

Group huddle In Antarctica, immense colonies of breeding king penguins stand together for protection against predators such as petrels, which steal eggs and chicks.

School assembly A school of fish has a better chance of finding food and mates. It can spot predators more effectively, and if attacked can split up and create confusion.

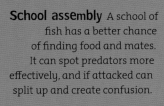

On the lookout

Meerkats live in large, highly organized groups. During the day, some will head out hunting, while others babysit the young or stand guard, barking a warning if they spot danger.

In the Kalahari Desert in South Africa, meerkats take turns to scan the landscape for potential predators.

Animal facts

1 Emperor penguins huddle in groups of up to 5,000 to survive Antarctic winters, which can get as cold as −76°F (−60°C).

2 When attacked or threatened, a minnow releases a chemical to warn other minnows of the danger.

3 In the Arctic, musk oxen will stand shoulder to shoulder to form a defensive barrier against attack by wolves.

Savanna survival The flat, treeless plains of Africa offer few hiding places for vulnerable animals. By grouping together, animals such as giraffes, zebras, springboks, and impalas have a better chance of avoiding attack.

TRICKS AND TRAPS

Sometimes a little bit of trickery goes a long way. Many animals have evolved clever camouflage or costumes to fool would-be attackers or prey. They are also excellent performers, capable of staying as still as a rock, stick, or flower, or even striking a pose that makes them appear dead and uninviting to predators.

An orb-weaving spider waits patiently for an insect to fly into its trap.

Dressed to kill

Camouflage is a powerful tool when hunting for a meal. Many creatures blend perfectly into their surroundings, enabling them to sneak up on prey or wait for prey to come to them. Their disguise is so convincing that their victim is totally fooled—right up until the last, fatal moment.

Arctic ghost The snowy owl's stunning white plumage blends in with its Arctic surroundings, which is very useful as it hunts during the day. Its prey includes lemmings, rabbits, rodents, birds, and fish.

Deadly stonefish Looking exactly like an algae-covered stone on a rocky reef, the stonefish is extremely dangerous. Spines on its dorsal fin inject the most toxic venom of any fish in the world.

 ## Animal facts

1 Scientists believe wobbegongs have been in our oceans for more than 160 million years.

2 Only the male snowy owl is all white. Female snowy owls are white with dark spots on their wings.

3 Not all camouflage is visual. For example, some animals roll in dung to disguise their scent.

Cunning hunter Wolves are intelligent predators, adapting their hunting methods to their surroundings. This timber wolf crouches low to the ground so the dry grass camouflages its gray fur.

Master of disguise

Masquerading as a flower, this pretty pink orchid mantis evades detection by predators but also attracts insects, which it devours.

Some insects have perfected the art of disguise, with a costume that fools both predator and prey.

Why do killer whales have white undersides?

Wobbegongs have lightning reflexes and dagger-sharp teeth.

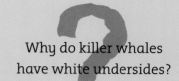

Wily wobbegong This shark is full of tricks. Its mottled skin blends in with the seafloor, while the tassels around its snout lure hungry fish. It lies perfectly still until it senses its prey, then pounces.

A: So sea creatures below cannot see them against the light of the sky.

Long jumper Instead of using leg muscles to jump, as humans do, jumping spiders propel themselves by altering the pressure of the liquid inside their body. Their excellent eyesight helps them judge jumping distances.

spider secrets

Spiders have an amazing collection of weapons to help them hunt. Camouflage, sharp fangs, poison, speed, mobility, finely tuned senses, and endless streams of strong and versatile silk enable them to overcome prey as small as a fly and as large as a human. This makes them fascinating as well as fearsome.

This spider is making a quick getaway on a strong line of silk called a dragline.

Master weavers

A strand of spider silk is elastic, but as strong as steel. It is incredibly useful. Spiders can use it to bind victims, move around, construct shelters, protect eggs, and build many different types of webs.

The scaffold web has vertical threads reaching the ground that trap insects walking past.

When prey blunders into a triangle web, the spider lets go of its end and the web collapses.

This hammock web traps prey in a sticky maze until it eventually falls onto a platform.

Booby trap The trapdoor spider waits until it feels the vibrations of its prey walking over its hidden door. Then it races up, raises its hatch, and pounces.

Scuba spider The diving bell spider builds its underwater home by trapping air inside a silken web. It preys on aquatic animals that pass by. It also goes out hunting, breathing from a thin film of air around its abdomen.

Flower power Some crab spiders can change colors like a chameleon. They sit on top of a flower, blending in perfectly. When an unsuspecting insect comes to collect nectar, it gets a nasty surprise!

Hiding in sight

Whether they live on land or in the sea, in deserts, lush rainforests, or snow-covered terrain, many animals use pattern or color to blend into the background. Cunning camouflage can help a creature avoid attracting the attention of predatory eyes—and becoming a victim.

Sticky surprise With its long, thin body, twiggy legs, and motionless posture, the stick insect is hard to spot. It looks like part of a tree branch.

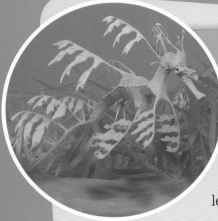

Hiding in the sea

Creatures can go unnoticed on the sandy seabed if they have speckled skin and a flat body and stay relatively still. Among vibrant coral, brighter colors work. Sea dragons are fish that have a different disguise: leafy appendages that look like seaweed.

The leafy sea dragon has yellow-green coloring and "fins" that look just like trailing seaweed.

Gobies are small fish. Discreet coloring helps them blend into the background.

This leopard flounder has a pattern that looks just like the pebbly ocean floor.

Which animal changes color the fastest?

The sloth moth lays its eggs in the sloth's dung.

ZOOM IN

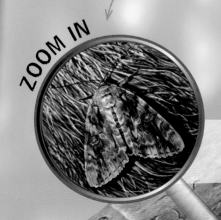

Insect impersonators

Brimstone butterfly
The veined, leaf-shaped wings
of this butterfly help it blend in
perfectly with its background.

Leaf mimic katydid A pile
of dead leaves on the forest
floor is the perfect refuge
for this insect.

Bark bug When motionless,
this little bug is almost
impossible to spot against
the bark of a tree.

Slothful living The three-toed
sloth is a slow-moving tree-dweller.
Green algae grows on its coat,
helping to camouflage it within
the leafy canopy.

The **sloth moth** lives in the sloth's shaggy fur.

A: The cuttlefish.

Clever copycats

Many animals defend themselves by using mimicry to trick predators or prey into thinking they are something else. Some display the same colors or patterns as a dangerous, poisonous, or bad-tasting animal. Others have a body part that makes it looks like another animal, which confuses or startles attackers and gives the animal a chance to escape.

Can you spot the differences between this ant and the spider below?

Ant or spider? The spider below is masquerading as a weaver ant. Weaver ants have a terrible taste and painful bite, so the spider's disguise fools predators into thinking it is just another unappetizing ant.

Why do male cuttlefish sometimes mimic female cuttlefish?

Black patches on the spider's head look like ant eyes.

The harmless milk snake copies the colors of the poisonous coral snake for protection.

Fake owl-eyes startle predators when the moth opens its wings.

Watchful wings
Eyespots on the wings of the polyphemus silk moth (far left) look just like the fierce gaze of an owl (left). The moth uses its spots to scare away hungry birds.

Copying this owl's piercing gaze is a clever survival strategy.

Animals recognize the colors of the nasty yellow jacket wasp and stay away.

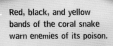

Red, black, and yellow bands of the coral snake warn enemies of its poison.

The wasp beetle copies the yellow jacket wasp for protection.

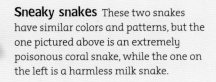

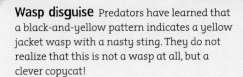

Sneaky snakes These two snakes have similar colors and patterns, but the one pictured above is an extremely poisonous coral snake, while the one on the left is a harmless milk snake.

Wasp disguise Predators have learned that a black-and-yellow pattern indicates a yellow jacket wasp with a nasty sting. They do not realize that this is not a wasp at all, but a clever copycat!

A: *So they can mate with females without other males detecting them.*

Faking it

When danger looms and escape is impossible, many animals will put on the performance of their life. Some drop their tail or a leg as a decoy or feign injury to distract their attackers. Others simply play dead. The more convincing their act, the better chance they have for survival.

Tricky tail Most lizard species, including geckos, can drop their tail when they are under attack. The tail keeps wriggling like a tasty worm, diverting the attacker's attention while the animal escapes.

The gecko escapes, leaving its wriggling tail behind. It then grows a new tail.

Plover's eggs

What does "playing possum" mean?

Broken wing Plovers and other ground-nesting birds sometimes fake an injured wing to convince predators they are easy pickings. They flap around on the ground and lead the predator away from their precious nest.

Animal facts

1 The tail of the Australian chameleon gecko not only wriggles after it is dropped, but also squeaks.

2 Lizards and spiders can regenerate their shed legs or tail over a number of weeks.

3 Darwin's frog of South America will jump into a stream and roll onto its back, playing dead while the water carries it away.

Playing dead

Most animals prefer to hunt and eat live prey, so some creatures will play dead to evade the attention of predators. Some will even release a smell similar to rotting meat.

This grass snake might look dead, but once the threat has passed, it will spring to life and slither safely away.

When it senses danger, the opossum feigns death, or "plays possum." Its eyes glaze over, its tongue hangs out, and its breathing slows down.

The **harvestman** can drop one of its legs to confuse a predator.

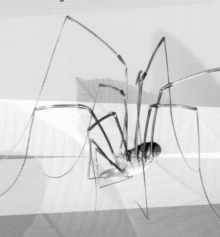

A: Pretending to be dead, unconscious, or asleep.

Fatal attraction

Not all predators actively seek out their prey. Some have perfected the art of attracting prey to them. With a few nifty tricks—such as clever camouflage and convincing lures—and a great deal of patience, these creatures have managed to take the hard physical work out of finding their next meal.

The heron drops a leaf or twig into the moving stream.

The heron follows its swirling lure downstream.

When a fish swims up to investigate, the hungry heron snatches it up.

Animal facts

1 The Australian bird-dropping spider looks and smells like bird dung, to attract its favorite food: flies.

2 Margay cats, from Central and South America, sometimes imitate the distress call of a young tamarin monkey to lure adult tamarins.

3 Some snakes use caudal luring to attract prey, wriggling and waving their tail until the prey comes within striking distance.

Bird bait Green herons have developed an innovative way of catching a meal. They carefully select sticks or leaves that are light enough to swirl on the water's surface and attract fish.

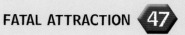

Lure

Gone fishing

Anglerfish are slow-moving predators that wait for food to come to them. They dangle a glowing or wormlike lure in front of their cavernous mouth, which draws unsuspecting prey within easy striking distance.

The deep-sea anglerfish uses its bright lure to attract hungry fish in the deep, dark ocean—then gobbles them down.

How does the *Portia* spider lure its spider prey?

Death trap

Perfectly camouflaged by its mud-brown, algae-covered shell, the alligator snapping turtle opens its mouth to reveal a tantalizing, wriggling, wormlike tongue. When a hungry fish ventures in ... wham!

A: *By plucking out the rhythm of a trapped insect on the spider's web.*

CHEMICAL WARFARE

Spines, spurs, saliva, tentacles, fangs, fur, and feathers—anything and everything has poisonous potential in the animal kingdom. Creatures use toxins to stun, paralyze, or kill outright, making it easier to devour prey or escape from an attacker. Unfortunately for the victim, the danger is often invisible—until it is too late!

A venomous sea krait lurks in the coral reef, ready to ambush prey.

Underwater assassins

Forget about sharks—the most deadly ocean creatures are far smaller and much more difficult to see. The blue-ringed octopus and the stonefish are two of the most poisonous animals in the world, but they are small and perfectly camouflaged. Some animals have learned to benefit from the ocean's assassins, but most just steer clear!

Lethal stone This is one stone you do not want to step on. The well-camouflaged stonefish carries deadly poisons, called neurotoxins, in the spines along its back. Its sting is strong enough to kill a human.

Toxic tentacles The Portuguese man-of-war is a floating death trap for small, unsuspecting sea creatures such as fish and shrimp. Its tentacles, which are usually about 32 feet (10 m) long, deliver venom via harpoon-like stinging cells called nematocysts.

Ocean killer The blue-ringed octopus is the most deadly sea creature in the world. It is only 5–8 inches (12–20 cm) long, but its bite can kill a human in minutes.

Behind anemone lines

Clown fish and sea anemones have a symbiotic relationship, which means each benefits from the other. The anemone's stinging tentacles protect the clown fish from predators, and the clown fish's excretions provide nutrients to the anemone.

The clown fish are immune to the sea anemone's poison, so they can live safely within its tentacles.

Warrior snail This seemingly innocent cone shell packs a powerful weapon: a radula, or mouthpart, that injects a dose of venom into its prey that is strong enough to kill or paralyze it.

Armed and dangerous When hunting, the cuttlefish will sometimes put on a mesmerizing display of patterns and colors along its tentacles to attract prey, before striking out with paralyzing venom.

Snakes alive!

Slithering, hissing, secretive, and stealthy, snakes understandably make many of us quake with fear. But snakes are also fascinating creatures. They have well-developed senses and the ability to survive and thrive in all sorts of environments—whether in water or on land, desert or rainforest, mountainous regions or flat plains.

Lightning strike
The golden eyelash viper waits in a tree and lashes out swiftly with a venomous bite. Its horny "eyelashes" protect its eyes as it moves through vegetation.

Super sensitive A snake's senses are finely tuned to help it locate and hunt prey. It also has something called a Jacobson's organ on the roof of its mouth, which enables it to analyze chemicals picked up by its flicking, forked tongue.

Special heat-sensitive pits behind the snake's nostrils help it locate prey.

The fangs are hinged so they can fold back into the snake's mouth.

The tongue takes samples of particles in the environment and passes information to the brain.

Animal facts

1 Snakes do not have external ears. Instead, they read vibrations using their inner ears.

2 Snake charmers do not hypnotize snakes with music, as snakes cannot hear it! Rather, the snake responds to the swaying motion of the flute.

3 Sea kraits can stay underwater for up to one hour.

Water snakes

There are two types of water-dwelling snakes: semiaquatic sea kraits and true sea snakes. Sea kraits lay their eggs on land, while true sea snakes live in the water and bear live young.

Sea snakes can close their nostrils to keep out water, and have paddle-like tails to help them swim.

How do snakes "see" their prey in the dark?

Strict diet The African egg-eating snake eats only eggs. It swallows the egg whole and breaks it using bony protrusions in its throat. Then it drains the egg and regurgitates the shell.

A: By sensing temperature changes in the air around them.

Spotlight on

rattlesnakes

The western diamondback rattlesnake can grow up to 4½ feet (1.5 m).

In the world of snakes, there is no clearer warning signal than the buzz of a rattlesnake's tail. Rattlesnakes are generally very well camouflaged in their environment, but if danger looms too close, they let their tails do the talking. All rattlesnakes have a venomous bite that can stun or kill prey within seconds.

Rough diamond Of the 33 species of rattlesnakes in the world, the diamondback is the biggest and most dangerous. It strikes with lightning speed and injects venom that destroys tissue and blood vessels.

Anatomy of a rattle

A rattlesnake's tail is made of a number of hollow, hard shells, or rings. When the snake shakes its tail, the rings knock against each other, creating a rattling sound.

Each time a rattlesnake sheds its skin, a new layer of hollow shells is formed.

The rattlesnake shakes its tail to frighten off predators or distract them from its venomous fangs while it prepares to strike.

Fangs swing forward when the rattlesnake opens its mouth to bite.

Ambush predator

A rattlesnake strikes with incredible speed, using its coiled, muscular body as a launching pad. Its head bursts forward and quickly delivers a large dose of venom via its fangs.

A protruding windpipe helps the snake breathe while it feeds on its prey.

Venomous mammals

There are nearly 5,000 mammal species in the world, and yet barely a dozen of them are venomous. Scientists are not sure why there are so few. Perhaps it is because they have evolved other effective methods of defense and attack. Whatever the reason, these are rare and special mammals indeed.

Animal facts

1 The solenodon is one of the most endangered mammals in the world.

2 Skunks and polecats release a toxic, foul-smelling substance from near their anus when threatened. It can cause skin irritation and blindness.

3 The slow loris spreads toxin onto the fur of its young, to protect them from predators.

This sharp spur is connected to a venom gland in the platypus's leg.

Shrewd customer
The Eurasian water shrew is one of two species of shrews known to inject venom via their saliva. This weapon comes in handy when taking down larger prey, such as fish or frogs.

Webbed warrior The platypus may appear quaint, with its furry body and ducklike bill, but it is actually a fierce fighter, with a venomous spur behind its webbed back feet that can inflict a paralyzing sting.

Nasty biter

The solenodon, a ratlike creature that is found only in Cuba, lives in burrows and hunts at night. Hidden within its impressively long snout is a fierce set of teeth that delivers a venomous bite.

The long, flexible snout is perfect for poking into small cracks and crevices in search of a tasty meal.

Venomous saliva comes through one of the solenodon's teeth in its lower jaw.

The solenodon hunts at night for insects, earthworms, and small invertebrates, immobilizing them with venom before devouring them.

Poisoned elbows The slow loris has an unusual method of poisoning its attackers: glands in its elbows produce a brown toxin, which it licks and mixes with its saliva. This makes its bite venomous!

What is a mole's most powerful sense?

Food stash If a mole catches more earthworms than it can eat, it paralyzes them with toxin in its saliva. It then stores the live worms in an underground "kitchen" until it is hungry again.

A: *Its sense of smell.*

Poisonous defense

Some animals are armed with a secret defensive weapon—poison! With a bite or even just a touch, they can release enough venom to immobilize, stun, or kill an attacker. Their poison comes in many different forms, from toxic feathers and skin to stinging hairs and deadly secretions.

Destructive force The cane toad is poisonous at every stage of its life: egg, tadpole, toadlet, and adult. Its poison oozes from glands on its shoulders, causing paralysis and cardiac arrest when ingested.

Acid attack Behind the puss moth caterpillar's charming and colorful costume lies a sinister defensive weapon: it sprays formic acid into the face of its attacker.

Why does the harmless viceroy butterfly mimic the colors and patterns of the monarch butterfly?

Poison feathers
The pitohui, which is found in New Guinea, is the only known poisonous bird in the world. The skin and feathers of some species, including this hooded pitohui, contain powerful toxins.

Warning colors The dazzling pattern on this blue-and-black poison-dart frog is typical of the species, and warns would-be attackers to keep away. These frogs come in all the colors of the rainbow.

Killer appetite Poison-dart frogs, such as the yellow-headed poison-dart frog, eat a special diet of arthropods to keep up their toxicity levels. Some tribes of Central and South America coat their arrow tips with the frogs' poison.

 ## Animal facts

1 The nonvenomous tiger keelback snake eats toxic toads and uses their poison to protect itself.

2 Doctors sometimes use the modified venom of rattlesnakes and vipers to treat strokes and heart attacks in humans.

3 The most poisonous frog in the world is the golden poison-dart frog. A small droplet of its poison is enough to kill up to 20 humans!

Milkweed plant

Deadly diet Monarch butterflies lay their eggs on milkweed plants as food for monarch caterpillars to eat. Milkweed contains toxins that make the adult butterflies poisonous if eaten.

A: To trick predators into thinking that it is poisonous.

Spitters and squirters

The element of surprise gives animals a supremely useful defensive edge when faced with an attacker. Some animals squirt, spray, regurgitate, and fire all sorts of weird and wonderful substances from different parts of their body—catching their attackers off-guard so they can make a quick getaway.

Stomach bomb
Southern giant petrels, like all albatrosses and petrels, extract oil from food and store it in their stomach. They use the oil for energy, to feed their young, or to regurgitate onto potential attackers.

Stinky spray When provoked, a skunk first raises its tail and stamps its feet as a warning. Then it emits a foul-smelling spray from glands in its rear, straight into its attacker's face.

Blood explosion Regal horned lizards have a bizarre method of defense: they squirt blood from behind their eyes to confuse predators. The squirt can reach up to 4 feet (1.2 m) and contains fluids that cause irritation.

What shimmering fabric is made from the saliva of a certain caterpillar?

Explosive attack When threatened, a bombardier beetle fires a spray of boiling-hot, noxious fumes and fluid from a chamber in its abdomen. The mixture is so explosive that it makes a bang.

The spitting spider traps flies with streams of sticky, paralyzing venom.

A: Silk, woven from the cocoon of the silkworm caterpillar.

Glossary

abdomen the part of an animal's body that contains the digestive system and organs of reproduction

ambush the act of attacking by surprise from a concealed or camouflaged position

anatomy the detailed structure of any part of an animal or plant

anesthetic a substance that causes loss of sensitivity in an animal, either by numbing a small area of its body or by rendering it unconscious

appendage any part of an animal that branches off from its main body

aquatic living or growing in water

arthropod a type of animal with a segmented body and jointed legs whose skeleton is on the outside of its body. Spiders and ants are arthropods.

asphyxiate to stop the intake of oxygen and release of carbon dioxide through breathing; to choke

camouflage body colors, patterns, or shapes that help an animal blend in with and stay hidden in its natural surroundings

canine teeth four pointed teeth, one on each side of each jaw, sitting between the front incisors and the side molars. Not all animals have canine teeth.

canopy the upper leafy branches of a tree or trees

carapace a shell-like cover on the back and sometimes front of an animal

cardiac arrest the stopping of blood pumping to and from the heart. Electric shocks, asphyxia, and some poisons can cause cardiac arrest.

carnivore an animal that eats the flesh of other animals

chameleon a type of lizard that can change the color of its skin to match its environment

colony a group of animals or plants of the same kind living together

congregate to gather together, often in a large group

constrictor a snake that kills by coiling around its prey

crustacean a type of animal, usually aquatic, whose body is covered by a hard outer covering, or shell. Lobsters, crabs, and shrimps are crustaceans.

decoy an artificial bait or lure, designed to entice an animal toward or away from something

dorsal describes a part of an animal's back

duct in an animal, a duct is a tube or canal through which a bodily fluid, such as a snake's venom, travels

excretions waste substances released by a plant or animal, such as urine, sweat, or feces

fibrous made up of a number of separate threadlike pieces

gland a part of the body that makes and releases (secretes) useful substances

herbivore an animal that eats only plants

hierarchy a system of ranking things in a certain order

impenetrable incapable of being broken into or entered

incisor teeth the teeth at the front part of the jaw that are used for fine work such as cutting flesh, or plucking feathers or hair from an animal carcass

ingest to put food into the body

invertebrates animals without backbones, such as jellyfish, spiders (whose skeletons are on the outside), and insects

keratin a type of protein found in human and animal skin and hair, as well as claws, nails, hooves, horns, and feathers

krill tiny, shrimplike sea creatures that live in large numbers in Arctic and Antarctic waters

mammals a group of animals that have hair or fur, are warm-blooded, and feed their young with milk

mandible the lower part of the jaw

masquerade a disguise

microsurgery surgery that is performed on extremely small parts of the body, such as veins and arteries

mimicry the act of mimicking or imitating something else

noxious harmful to health

order a subdivision of plants and animals

parasite a plant or animal that survives by extracting nutrients from another plant or animal

pectoral describes a part of an animal's chest

pedipalps appendages near the mouth of an arachnid such as a spider or scorpion, used as weapons or to help with feeding

plumage a bird's feathers

pod a collective term for animals, usually seals or whales

pores tiny openings in an animal's skin, or on the surface of a leaf

predator an animal that survives by hunting, killing, and eating other animals

prehistoric belonging to a period before recorded history

prey an animal or animals that are hunted, killed, and eaten by other animals

primates mammals belonging to the order Primates. Examples include humans, monkeys, chimpanzees, and gorillas.

protrusion something that projects from, or sticks out of, something else

raptor a bird of prey, such as an eagle, hawk, or owl

reflex an immediate, often involuntary, physical response to a stimulus

regurgitate to bring back food that has been fully or partially digested

remnant a small remaining trace of something

savanna a type of landscape characterized by flatness and sparse vegetation dominated by grasses. These landscapes are usually found in hot places, such as Africa.

school a group of fish

spurs sharp, clawlike structures on the legs of some birds and mammals

urethra the tube through which urine passes from the bladder

versatile capable of doing different tasks easily

vertebrates animals with backbones, such as humans, dogs, and whales

Index

The publisher thanks Puddingburn Publishing Services for the index.

Credits

Key tl=top left; t=top; tc=top center; tr=top right; cl=center left; c=center; cr=center right; bl=bottom left; bc=bottom center; br=bottom right; bg = background

CBCD = Kodak Photo Disc; CBT = Corbis; GI = Getty Images; iS = istockphoto.com; NHPA = Photoshot; SH = Shutterstock; TPL = photolibrary.com

PHOTOGRAPHS
Front Cover br, cr CBT; **Back Cover** tl iS; 1tr iS; 2bl iS; 3c CBT; br iS; 4cl iS; 5tr GI; 6-7c CBT; 8-9bg iS; 11bg CBCD; br CBT; tc iS; tl SH; 12bl, tr iS; 16bl, br, tr iS; tr SH; 16-17c iS; 17tc CBT; tl iS; 18tl iS; br, cl, cr TPL; 19c GI; tc TPL; 20c TPL; 20-21bc, tc GI; 21tl GI; br iS; 22-23c CBT; 24bl CBT; 28bl CBT; cl GI; 29tl CBT; 30cr GI; 32bc, cl, tr iS; 32-33cr iS; 33tc iS; 34-35c CBT; 36br, cl, tr iS; 38tr iS; 40bl SH; 41tl SH; 42bl, c iS; 42-43bg iS; 43cr, tc iS; 44tr NHPA; 44-45bg iS; 45cl, tr CBT; br iS; 48-49c CBT; 51tl iS; 52tr GI; 52-53bg iS; 53br GI; 54cl, tc iS; 56-57bc GI; bg iS; 57cl CBT; br iS; 58cl CBT; 58-59bg, tc iS; 58tr iS; bc NHPA; 59tl, tr iS; 60c CBT; tr iS; 62tl CBCD; tl NHPA

ILLUSTRATIONS
Peter Bull Art Studios 27br, 47t; Leonello Calvetti 14t, 24r; Barry Croucher/The Art Agency 14bl, 37, 54-55; Christer Eriksson 9, 10tl, 17r, 25; 41cr, 47; Gary Hanna/The Art Agency 26-27, 53t; Steve Hobbs 41t, 59, 61; Ian Jackson/The Art Agency 8bl, 10 bl, 10b, 40b, 50t, tr; David Kirshner 52-53; MBA Studios 26, 28-29; Terry Pastor/The Art Agency 60bl; Sandra Pond/The Art Agency 57tr; Mick Posen/The Art Agency 8tr, 14-15, 40cl, 46l, 50-51; Kevin Stead 21r, 56; Claude Thivierge/Contact Jupiter 11t, 11tr; Kim Thompson/Kingpin 17t, 42-43; Guy Troughton 44